FL🌸WERING

Easygoing
Floral
Design for
Surprising
Contemporary
Arrangements

ELIZABETH JAIME
founder of Calma Floral

PHOTOGRAPHY BY
EMMA FISHMAN

CHRONICLE BOOKS
SAN FRANCISCO

Library of Congress Cataloging-in-Publication
Data available.

ISBN 978-1-7972-2127-4

Manufactured in China.

Editing by Claire Gilhuly.
Design by Lizzie Vaughan.
Typesetting by Taylor Roy.

10 9 8 7 6 5 4 3 2 1

Chronicle books and gifts
are available at special quantity
discounts to corporations, professional
associations, literacy programs, and other
organizations. For details and discount information,
please contact our premiums department at
corporatesales@chroniclebooks.com or at
1-800-759-0190.

Chronicle Books LLC
680 Second Street
San Francisco, California 94107
www.chroniclebooks.com

TO MY ABUELA VIVIAN,

who never got to see this book in its completion. Without her,
this book would not have been possible, as she taught me
everything I know about creating things with my hands.

& TO MY MOM, ALSO VIVIAN,

who never fails to be an example of strength
and dedication and a source of support.

CONTENTS

I.

THE BASICS

54

II.
LET'S MAKE SOME ARRANGEMENTS

194

III.
RESOURCES + TIPS

When people ask me how I became a florist, I think they expect some sort of graceful story that involves hours of me flipping through flower books, expensive courses, and some sort of apprenticeship under a seasoned florist. Perhaps if that had been my reality, my path to floristry might have looked and felt a little less chaotic. But the truth is that I became a florist partly out of boredom and partly out of needing to figure out what the next phase of my life would look like.

It was January 2019, and I had just left my job as a visual editor at *Bon Appétit*, a job I loved but felt I had grown out of. I decided it was time to leave New York (as one eventually does), the city I had called home for nine years, and relocate to the place where I was born and raised, Miami.

I spent the first few months in Miami regretting my decision, mostly because I didn't really know what I was going to do for work. My identity in New York was closely tied to my profession, and in Miami I found myself without the community I was used to and without a job. So to pass the time, I began doing the things I loved, one of which was playing with flowers.

When I first started making flower arrangements, I truly had no idea what I was doing. I didn't know the names of any flowers, and I especially didn't know the tools and mechanisms needed to make sure my arrangements had movement, life, and structure. I was forced to figure that all out—and quickly— when I scored my first real flower gig, doing the arrangements for the beauty brand Glossier's Miami pop-up. Now, anyone who is familiar with Glossier knows how much emphasis they put on their retail florals, and to say that I was a little bit stressed would be an understatement. I felt scared and wholly unprepared. My fear was only heightened by my middle-of-the-night stress spirals where I imagined all the flowers dying within the first twenty-four hours (why does everything feel so much worse at 3 a.m. than it actually is?). I spent the month leading up to the job watching every YouTube video, checking out out-of-date flower guides from the library, and scouring blogs and Reddit posts trying to find all the answers I needed. And while I was able to find some of the information I sought, most of the knowledge I have today I've gathered from trial, error, and simply doing.

The Glossier job went so much better than I ever expected, but I realized I still had so much to learn. I spent the next year learning by doing and growing as a florist. I could have gone to a flower school (helpful, but unnecessary, if you ask me), or maybe worked under another florist (super helpful if you're young and at the beginning of your career), but I felt pretty confident that I had a good thing going and that if I just continued, I'd figure it out as I went.

Still, as this was happening, I wished there was an easy-to-follow guide for the type of flower arrangements I was interested in making. Everything I found was either too niche to one specific area of floristry or way too traditional. I decided then that once I had the knowledge and experience myself, I would write the book I was looking for. A few years later, and here we are.

Geared toward anyone who loves the idea of making flower arrangements but doesn't know where to start, this book is meant to take what I've learned along the way and demystify the art of arranging flowers. It also invites you to think outside the box and reimagine what a floral arrangement might look like. Putting aside traditional flower rules and leaning into an irreverent new wave of floral design, we'll work with unlikely materials and consider fun, unusual floral pairings that make a bold statement. I want you to flip through this book and feel inspired to create your own floral-arranging world that feels untethered to rules (well, most of them!) and finds you in your kitchen at 1 a.m. gluing rhinestones to an orchid for no other reason than because it looks so damn cool.

If you've ever leafed through a cookbook, you might find some familiarity in the format here. The first half of this book walks you through all the basic tools, principles, and ideas you'll need to familiarize yourself with in order to create beautiful, long-lasting arrangements. Some of these are nonnegotiable, like making sure to process your flowers. Some are just based on personal taste—like how I think chicken wire is the best flower mechanic for everyday use. Regardless, I've tried to reduce the noise and share only the essentials, because it really shouldn't be as complicated as some people make it out to be.

In the second half of the book, we'll get into the fun bit, where we look at actual arrangements and I show you exactly how to make each one. Just like a recipe, each arrangement includes a flower shopping list of ingredients, flower recipe instructions, and step-by-step photos of how I created each arrangement. The intention is for you to digest how I built each arrangement and feel inspired to create your own version. We'll also take a look at a few different types of arrangements and the best times to use them.

So whether you're interested in becoming a florist or just looking to elevate your at-home floral game, you'll learn that with a few foundational principles, some confidence, and the right set of tools, you too can make cool modern flower arrangements. Because it's really not as hard as it looks, and if I could teach myself how to make them, so can you.

I.
THE
BASICS

At the foundation of any flower arrangement are a few basic principles and techniques that apply regardless of what style of arrangement you're creating. Think of these as the building blocks that allow your arrangement to have a fun, modern shape and a good foundation and to last as long as possible.

When it comes to the basic rules, the amount of information out there can feel overwhelming and disheartening. So many vases! So many tools! *Where do I start?* It's dizzying and off-putting. For that reason, I've really edited down that information here. This section presents only the essentials that I come back to day after day as a professional florist.

THE TOOLS

One of the best things about taking up flower arranging as either
a hobby or a profession is that you really don't need a lot to get started.
At the bare minimum, a vase and some scissors are enough to get
you going. Still, there are a few tools that you can add to your arsenal
that will make things a little bit easier for you. And because I know
everyone's budget and interest level varies, I've divided this section
into two camps: one for those who are just dabbling, and the other for
those who are looking to take things to the next level. Whichever camp
you are in right now, don't feel the need to drop a lot of money on expensive
versions of any of the mentioned tools, because they'll 100 percent get
worn out and, if you're anything like me, also get lost from time to time.

For those who want to keep it bare-bones, all you really need is two essential tools.

Shears: You'll need a pair of flower shears to cut stems, and you'll want those blades to be sharp. Yes, plain old scissors might work (depending on how sharp they are!), but cutting stems over and over again might dull and dirty your at-home scissors, so having a dedicated pair of shears is a good idea. There are many different kinds of shears out there—some are made for thicker, woodier stems, while daintier shears are best for delicate flowers. For everyday flower arranging, just a basic pair of shears will work; it's what I use about 99 percent of the time.

As an alternative, some people prefer to use a flower knife instead of shears, and you might too! Shears are generally safer and more beginner friendly. I personally prefer them, as I tend to be a bit clumsy.

Clear floral tape: While not the most secure of all the mechanics we'll cover in this book, clear floral tape is definitely the cheapest, easiest to source, and most bare-bones, and that's why I'm including it in Just Dabbling. Without any other mechanics, clear floral tape is essential to holding plant material in place inside a vase. Regular tape won't work here; you need floral tape, as it's waterproof and made specifically for flower arranging. (Floral tape will also come in handy when working with different floral mechanics, like chicken wire, page 26.)

When shopping for tape, you might find green floral tape, which is equally helpful! The only difference is that green tape is more noticeable when working with white and light-colored vases and might be visible in your finished arrangement.

TAKE IT TO THE NEXT LEVEL ★★

For those who want to build out their flower toolbox a bit, add the following tools.

Lazy Susan: It's amazing how such a simple tool can make flower arranging so much easier. A lazy Susan is the perfect base for building arrangements on, as it allows you to easily spin your piece to get a good look at all sides and angles. Don't worry about getting anything fancy, as it's bound to get scratched up and wet—a cheap one from a big-box or home store will work just fine.

Watering can with a long, thin spout: Even though one of the first steps to building an arrangement is to add water to the vase, there are inevitably instances when you'll need to add water after an arrangement has been built. Things happen! Maybe you spilled some water from your arrangement as you were transporting it, or perhaps your day-old arrangements need refreshing, as the flowers drank more water than you expected. Finding a gap in your arrangement to add water through can be challenging; this is where a watering can with a long, thin spout comes in handy. It makes it really easy to add water without disturbing your blooms or the shape of your arrangement.

Floral clay: This waterproof putty is really important when working with certain flower mechanics like kenzans and flower frogs (which we'll get to on page 28), as it allows you to anchor the mechanic to the vase or other surface.

Floral buckets: Buckets aren't totally necessary, but they are extremely helpful when working with a large quantity of flowers. Having a couple of water-filled flower buckets nearby as you start to unpack and process your flowers allows you to stay organized

while also keeping your flowers hydrated. Otherwise, you might find yourself scrounging for random vases to hold all your processed flowers. Most florists use buckets from any home supply store, so don't feel the need to go out and look for special branded buckets. You may also be able to score free buckets from grocery store florist sections that would otherwise be discarded.

Water tubes: Water tubes are necessary when placing blooms anywhere that's not a vase. You'll most likely use these for an installation or a tablescape that has flowers scattered throughout.

It's really important that you thoroughly clean your buckets in between each use. Bacteria can easily build up, which will negatively affect the lifespan of your flowers. I use dish soap and a splash of bleach to clean my buckets.

THINGS YOU PROBABLY WON'T NEED

There are a dozen other products I could have included in this tool list, but you probably won't need them, and I'd feel bad asking you to waste your money. Even as a professional florist, I hardly use any of these.

Floral wire: Wiring flowers is tricky, and unless you are making boutonnieres and corsages for a wedding, chances are you'll rarely need to use floral wire.

Glue: I've seen hot glue and cold glue on a lot of lists, but to this day I have never had to glue any flowers. Skip this one!

Thorn stripper: Unless you're working with roses very often, don't waste your money on a thorn stripper.

Flower food: There tend to be two camps of florists: those who use flower food and those who don't. There's a lot of debate as to how helpful flower food is in extending the life of your flowers. Personally, I do not use flower food, as I haven't noticed much of a difference when I *have* used it.

A Note on Trash

Working with flowers creates a lot of trash. More than I ever could have imagined. First, there's all the packaging that purchased flowers come in: plastic sleeves, twist ties, cotton sleeves, and cardboard boxes. Then there's all the floral waste, like leaves and stems. If you want your workspace to stay clean and organized, I highly recommend having a large trash can nearby lined with a heavy-duty trash bag. Bonus points if you also keep a compost bin for natural waste!

MECHANICS

Okay, here's where I get a little bit serious. Not in a militant, you-absolutely-need-to-do-this kind of way but in a this-is-going-to-make-your-life-so-much-easier kind of way. Mechanics are here to make creating flower arrangements much simpler for you.

Mechanics are the tools and objects that enable you to create structure and stability in your arrangements, ultimately making it easier for you to make the kind of arrangements that look effortlessly cool. Without some sort of mechanic to hold your flowers in place, your stems will be flopping all over, leaving you frustrated, disheartened, and wondering if flower arranging is just not for you. If a successful arrangement seems perfectly thrown together in a laissez-faire kind of way, you know it's using mechanics! Every single arrangement I create has some sort of flower mechanic in it to ensure that the flowers are staying where I want them to. New materials and methods come and go, but here are some of my favorites and the ones I turn to over and over again.

CHICKEN WIRE

Chicken wire is without a doubt the flower mechanic I use the most. It's easy to use, it's inexpensive compared to other mechanics, and it provides a sturdy structure for arrangements. Florist-grade chicken wire is resistant to rusting, but for everyday use, normal chicken wire from any garden supply store works too. When you're first starting out, it might not feel like enough support for your flimsy stems, but with practice, any flower lover will find chicken wire to be one of the best floral mechanics available.

HOW TO USE

1. Cut a rectangular piece of chicken wire about double the size of the opening of the vase.

2. Take opposite corners of the chicken wire and twist the ends together. You should be left with a shape that resembles a cannoli.

3. Scrunch the chicken wire cannoli and push it down into the vase. This will 100 percent alter the shape of your chicken wire cannoli, and that's okay! All that scrunching is creating different nooks and crannies for your flower stems to lean on. Once pushed in, the chicken wire should feel snugly wedged into the vase (meaning, if you shake the vase, the chicken wire shouldn't really be moving around). The top of the chicken wire should be flush with the lip of the vase, if not hanging over just a tiny bit.

4. Use clear floral tape in an X formation on top of the vase to secure the chicken wire in place.

5. Add water to the vase.

6. Begin arranging the flowers, wedging stems into different gaps and spaces in the chicken wire.

FLOWER TAPE GRID

Flower tape grids come in handy when working with a glass vase, where you would otherwise see the chicken wire or kenzan. I don't recommend tape grids if you're just starting out, because it can be tricky to get your flowers to stay in place using this method. (I rarely use flower tape grids, mainly because I rarely use glass vases. The kinds of arrangements I like to create need the structure of a heavy-duty mechanic to stay in place.) Still, sometimes you have to use a glass vase, for whatever reason, and that's when a clear flower tape grid comes in handy.

HOW TO USE

1. Lay a piece of tape across the width of the vase, leaving at least 2 in [5 cm] of tape down the sides. Lay another piece of tape perpendicular to the first, creating an X.

2. Keep laying pieces of tape until you've created a grid.

3. Insert stems through the gaps.

Floral Foam → I won't lie to you: I've used floral foam before. I'm not proud to say it, because using foam is not eco-conscious. When I first started making arrangements, I was mostly using floral foam. At the time, I thought it was the only way to create structured, modern arrangements, and I didn't realize there were other mechanics I could use to achieve the same look without negatively impacting the environment. Look, much of the global flower industry is pretty bad for the environment, but it's no secret that floral foam is especially bad, given that it's made of tiny little single-use microplastics that never break down. So, while I'm not here to shame you for using foam, I am here to tell you that there's absolutely no reason to. You can achieve the same look and sturdiness with other, more eco-friendly floral mechanics.

KENZANS + FLOWER FROGS

Kenzans, sometimes called flower frogs, are another personal favorite of mine, but beware—they're expensive! A kenzan is a heavy metal disk with spiky needles sticking up from the metal base. A kenzan is affixed to the inner bottom of your vase using flower clay or putty. Stems are pushed directly onto the needles to keep them standing upright. A kenzan can be a bit of a balancing act—too much weight on one side, and you might find the vase toppling over—so learning to use this mechanic takes practice and patience. Because of how expensive kenzans can be, I use them only for arrangements I make for myself or for instances when I know I'll be able to get my kenzans back.

HOW TO USE

1. Find a vase with a wide-enough base to support the kenzan, which should be affixed to a completely flat surface. You can also affix kenzans directly onto surfaces (as in Carnations + Candles, page 157).

2. Create a disk of floral putty about one-quarter the size of the kenzan. Use the putty to secure the kenzan to the bottom of the vase or surface.

3. Add water to the vase.

4. Insert stems as you wish, making sure to really dig those stems deep into the spikes to secure them.

5. When I know I'm going to be creating an arrangement with tall or heavy blooms, I'll use both chicken wire and a kenzan as my mechanics. To do this, simply follow the steps in securing a kenzan to the bottom of the vase and then add a ball of chicken wire on top.

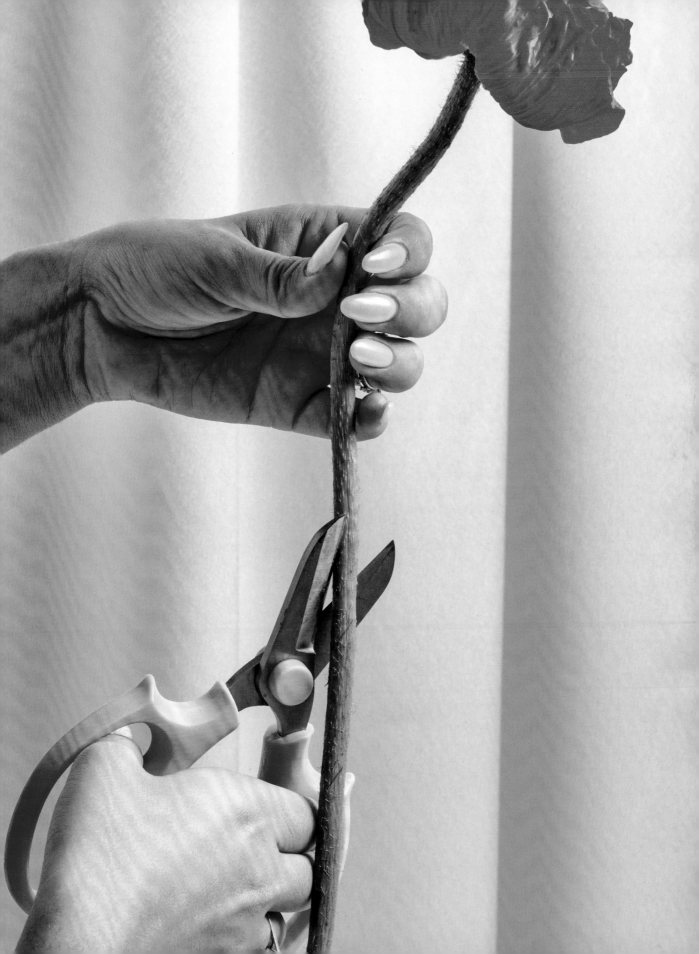

VESSELS + VASES

NONWATERTIGHT VESSELS

Every once in a while you might come across the most beautiful vessel or vase that is, sadly, not watertight. I find this to be the case for a lot of raw earthenware vases that haven't been sealed or fired. And while I would rarely recommend displaying flowers without a water source, there's a quick and inexpensive workaround for this. Find a glass cylinder vase (often called a hurricane glass) that is just 1 or 2 in [2.5 or 5 cm] smaller in dimension (height and width) than your nonwatertight vase. Create your arrangement in the hurricane glass and then just slip the hurricane glass into the opening of the nonwatertight vase. The hurricane glass will be concealed inside, and unless someone nosy peers down into the vase, chances are everyone will just assume you created the arrangement directly in the nonwatertight vase.

It's time to reconsider what you might think of as a vase. In my opinion, just about any watertight container that can hold at least 2 in [5 cm] of water will function as a flower vessel. So while a beautiful, expensive vase is always nice to have (and makes for a really great gift!), there's really no need to drop tons of cash to create irreverent, distinctive, stunning arrangements. On the contrary, I believe that the simpler the vase, the more room you leave for your flowers and arrangements to shine. That's why you'll very rarely see me using ornate, complicated vessels, as I find that they have a tendency to steal the show—and of course, I'm all about the flowers. Still, it's important to be familiar with the different types of flower vessels, because the shape and size of the vase can greatly affect the shape, flow, and presentation of your arrangement. In the same vein, it can be helpful to know when to use a certain type of flower vessel to dictate the overall look and feel of an arrangement.

BOWLS

When I tell people that I buy some of my favorite flower vessels at Target and West Elm, they automatically think that I must be shopping in their plant and flower sections. But I'm not! I'm actually buying bowls from their kitchen and dining section. Yes, like actual pasta and soup bowls! You might be surprised to hear that a lot of your favorite florists are doing the same. Pasta and soup bowls make for great low-profile flower vessels that also feel chic, given that they're often made of ceramic. If you decide to use a bowl, just make sure you're using one with a wide, sturdy base to avoid having your arrangements tip over!

PROS

○ Wide opening allows for wide, sprawling arrangements.

○ Low-profile vessel doesn't add more visual noise to already-busy arrangements.

○ They're wallet-friendly and easy to source.

CONS

✕ Not great for transport; they can easily tip over if not secured correctly.

✕ Less space for water means having to refill water more often.

BEST FOR

360 ARRANGEMENTS

FORWARD-FACING ARRANGEMENTS

BEST MECHANICS TO USE

KENZAN

CHICKEN WIRE METHOD

WHERE I LIKE TO SOURCE

HOME DECOR STORES LIKE CB2, WEST ELM, TARGET

VINTAGE SHOPS

SEE THEM IN USE

A WHIMSICAL, FLOSSY CLOUD
page 61

SHE'S FLIRTY, SHE'S FUN
page 69

TROPICAL(ISH)²
page 75

JUICY SUNBURST
page 87

A TROPICAL DELIGHT
page 95

ALL ABOUT ALLIUMS
page 101

WILD + MOSSY MOUNDS FOR A DINNER TABLE
page 163

BUD VASES + EXTRA SMALL VASES

The term "bud vase" can mean a lot of different things, but I consider a bud vase to be any small vessel with a 1 to $3\frac{1}{2}$ in [2.5 to 9 cm] opening. Bud vases are often used to create small floral arrangements with just a few stems. Depending on the size of the vase opening, you may or may not need mechanics. Either way, bud vases are a simple and efficient way to create a bunch of tiny arrangements or a small, single-flower moment.

PROS

○ Easy to arrange

○ Don't require a lot of flowers

○ Wallet-friendly and easy to source

○ Easy to transport

CONS

✕ Not great for creating a "wow" moment

✕ Can be difficult to create sprawling arrangements

BEST FOR

COMPLEMENTING LARGER ARRANGEMENTS ON A LONG TABLE

CREATING SMALL FLOWER MOMENTS THROUGHOUT THE HOUSE; FOR EXAMPLE, ON A BEDSIDE TABLE OR IN A POWDER ROOM

CREATING A VISUAL FRENZY OF FLOWERS EN MASSE AND WITH VARYING HEIGHTS

BEST MECHANICS TO USE

CHICKEN WIRE METHOD

NO MECHANICS—WITH SMALL-OPENING BUD VASES, YOU MIGHT NOT NEED ANY

WHERE I LIKE TO SOURCE

HOME DECOR STORES LIKE CB2, WEST ELM, TARGET

VINTAGE SHOPS

ETSY

YOUR CUPBOARD (JUST ABOUT ANYTHING CAN FUNCTION AS A BUD VASE; SEE PAGE 149)

SEE THEM IN USE

ANATOMY OF A BUD VASE
page 135

GOOD THINGS COME IN THREES
page 143

ANYTHING CAN BE A VASE MÉLANGE
page 149

TALL + NARROW VASES

Tall, narrow vases are your friend when you're trying to create arrangements with height and verticality. Because of the vase's small, narrow interior, your stems will have to lean at a shallower angle, therefore creating taller, more vertical flower moments. These are perfect for entryways and arrangements that need to live on the floor, and when grouped together with smaller arrangements to create dimension and variation in height. There's also something very chic about placing just a few stems of large branches in a tall vase and calling it a day!

PRO

⚬ Can be simple to arrange with when using just a few stems or a single variety

⚬ Easy to create a "wow" moment given how large they can be

CONS

✕ Not easy to transport (you might find yourself having to place the vase in the passenger seat of your car and strap it in with the seat belt!)

✕ Will require longer-stemmed flowers and branches

BEST FOR

ENTRYWAY FLORAL MOMENTS

SINGLE-FLOWER-VARIETY ARRANGEMENTS

A SIMPLE, LUSH GREENERY MOMENT WITH BIG TROPICAL LEAVES

ARRANGEMENTS THAT NEED TO BE PLACED ON THE FLOOR

GRAPHIC ARRANGEMENTS WITH MINIMAL SPREAD

WHERE I LIKE TO SOURCE

HOME DECOR STORES LIKE CB2, WEST ELM, TARGET

VINTAGE SHOPS

ETSY

SEE THEM IN USE

ON BIG ISLAND TIME
page 115

SWINGING AMARANTH
page 127

BEST MECHANICS TO USE

CHICKEN WIRE METHOD

TAPE METHOD

NO MECHANICS—WITH SMALL-OPENING TALL VASES, YOU MIGHT NOT NEED ANY

CYLINDER VASES

Because they're available in a variety of materials, colors, and sizes, I consider a cylinder vase to be any type of vessel where the base is as wide as the opening. Given their ease of use (they are very stable) and how easy they are to source (you'll find them at any floral supply or craft store), cylinder vases are perfect for beginner florists who are just starting to find their groove and looking to experiment and develop their own style. Even as you graduate to more challenging vessels, cylinder vases will probably remain in your arsenal—I use them for my delivery orders because they're easy to transport and aren't too expensive.

PROS

⚬ Beginner-friendly, in that the basic shape allows for differently shaped arrangements and exploration

⚬ Great for gifting, as you can find inexpensive cylinder vases

⚬ Easy to transport

CON

✕ Can be difficult to create an arrangement that has a lot of spread, as the higher walls of the vase don't allow the stems to fan out as much

BEST FOR

MAKING AN ARRANGEMENT AS A GIFT

ARRANGEMENTS THAT NEED TO BE TRANSPORTED

A SIMPLE FLOWER ARRANGEMENT THAT YOU DON'T WANT TO SPEND TOO MUCH TIME SETTING UP

BEST MECHANICS TO USE

CHICKEN WIRE METHOD

TAPE METHOD

KENZAN

WHERE I LIKE TO SOURCE

HOME DECOR STORES LIKE CB2, WEST ELM, TARGET

VINTAGE SHOPS

ETSY

SEE THEM IN USE

REFLEXED ROSE EXPLOSION
page 81

PINK GINGER PUNCH
page 107

TALL AND NARROW

BOWL

BOWL

TALL AND NARROW

BUD VASE

TALL AND NARROW

CYLINDER

BOWL

DESIGNER DISH

PREPPING + PROCESSING YOUR FLOWERS

I was really naïve in thinking that the flowers we buy from farmers' markets, grocery stores, or even wholesalers are 100 percent prepped and ready for arranging. No matter where you source them, all flowers need really good prep in order to live as long as possible in an arrangement. Florists refer to this preparation of flowers as processing. Processing is a sometimes tedious but necessary step that should not be overlooked. Every flower that comes into my studio undergoes the same level of processing. Think about it this way: By the time the flowers come into your possession, they likely have traveled quite a distance. While the methods of transporting flowers are highly technical and specialized, your flowers will likely arrive thirsty and a little bit sad. Processing your flowers encourages them to perk back up and put on their best show.

HOW TO PROCESS YOUR FLOWERS

1.

2.

Fill a very clean bucket or vase (or several, depending on how many flowers you're processing) with room-temperature water. Unwrap the flowers from any packaging. Remove any rubber bands or ties.

Remove the leaves. How many leaves you remove is up to you. I tend to take most leaves off, and if I ever leave any, it's just a few up close to the bloom. Whatever you do, make sure there are never any leaves submerged in the water. Leaves in water can create bacteria that will affect the lifespan of your flowers.

3.

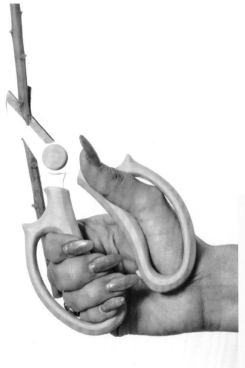

4.

Give the stems a fresh cut at a diagonal, which creates a larger surface area for water absorption.

Place the stems in the water-filled bucket or vase. While it's not necessary, it is best to keep flowers of the same length grouped together so that there aren't any short blooms getting squished by larger, bushier stems.

POPPIES NEED
A LITTLE MORE LOVE

Poppies usually come with buds encased. Removing the encasing will allow the flower to bloom quickly. To do so, find a slight crack in the encasing and use your fingers to gently peel it off.

Poppies contain a sap that allows them to more easily retain their moisture. When you cut poppies, the sap has a tendency to seep out. To create a seal that locks in the sap, sear the cut ends with a lit match for about 10 seconds.

FLOWER GLOSSARY

I want you to change the way you look at plant material when shopping for flowers. If you're anything like me, you might walk into a flower shop and want to buy absolutely everything and anything that catches your eye. While that can be really fun (and I do encourage doing that from time to time), it can also be overwhelming, and you might end up buying more flowers than you actually need. Knowing what kind of flowers to buy, and how to arrange them, will ultimately help you build better flower arrangements at home. So instead of buying a flower simply because you think it looks pretty (you can still marvel at its beauty—just later!), I want you to think about what quality or attribute any given flower might bring to your arrangement. For example, I look to taller-stemmed flowers, such as anthuriums, to add height to low, rounded arrangements. On the flip side, large focal blooms, such as peonies, often help ground and add volume to taller or sparser arrangements. The Flower Glossary that follows introduces you to some of my favorite flowers and sorts them into groups that help explain when and why I choose to use a specific flower.

Some of the flowers in this glossary could technically fall into two categories, such as anthuriums, which double as a Tall Boy and a Showstopper. Or carnations, which can act as a floral-forward Filler or even a Showstopper (for those daring enough to look past the unfair stereotype that carnations are a cheap, low-end flower). I've placed each flower in the category I think is most fitting, but feel free to experiment and look past any single attribute.

SHOPPING FOR FLOWERS

Before we get started, you should know that one of the most frustrating parts of working with flowers is shopping for and sourcing them. Mostly because in the age of social media, it's so easy to see an amazing arrangement with the most unusual flowers and want to recreate it using those exact blooms. But chances are, unless you're living in a major city like New York, Los Angeles, London, or Paris, each with world-famous flower markets, it's going to be difficult to find the specific flowers you saw online. It took me a long time to accept that, and I wish someone had been honest with me from the start! It would have saved me countless hours sending emails to New York wholesalers begging them to FedEx me some specific flower (don't make my mistake; it's really expensive, and they don't always survive the trip), not to mention sad attempts at trying to convince my local wholesaler that they need to be carrying such-and-such flower.

A couple different factors influence flower availability. First is **location**. Where you're located will heavily dictate what flowers you have access to. If you're in a major city, chances are there is a flower wholesale market that serves as a hub for floral suppliers in the surrounding areas. Flowers are flown in to those hubs—mostly from South and Central America and Europe, the epicenters of the cut-flower-growing industries—and then sold to florists and other consumers. If you're in a smaller city, your options may be somewhat limited, given that you're not close to one of those hubs. In those cases, there are a few options you could explore.

Where to Shop for Flowers

■ Seek out local flower farmers who sell cut flowers. **You may not have a wide selection to choose from (flower farmers have to work with the seasons, and some grow only a few varieties), but there's something really special about working with locally grown, just-cut stems. If your city has a good farmers' market, you might be able to find locally grown flowers there too. Flowers from local flower farms are always the freshest and less expensive, and they're better for the environment!**

■ Buy from your local flower shop. **Flower shops often have what's commonly referred to as a stem bar—a section of the shop where you can purchase bunches of flowers and even single stems.**

■ Purchase flowers at your local grocery store. **While they may not have the most unusual selection of flowers to choose from, grocery stores are a good place to buy flowers in a pinch. Just make sure to inspect the flowers before buying them! Look closely and choose the freshest flowers that still look perky and have no browning.**

■ Buy your flowers online. **There are online floral suppliers who allow you to shop online and then ship your flowers to you. Often, though, you'll have to buy a pretty large quantity, so I recommend this option to those who will need a lot of flowers at once.**

The second factor to consider when sourcing flowers is **seasonality**. Contrary to popular belief, outside of common and greenhouse-raised flowers—such as roses, carnations, and lilies—a lot of flowers are still grown according to season, meaning their availability changes throughout the year. That's why I sometimes have to let a client know that it will be impossible for me to include a dahlia in any arrangements made in February. Or why you're probably going to have a hard time finding poppies in the heat of summer.

I've found that these limitations on what flowers I have access to actually push me to be creative and find fun solutions that make my flower arrangements special in their own way. Once I came to accept that I wasn't going to have access in Miami to the same flowers as my New York floral peers, or that I couldn't control the flower seasons, I learned how to make arrangements that still felt different and exciting, using the flowers I *did* have access to. In the same spirit, you shouldn't feel put off from flower arranging just because you have access to only the flowers sold at your local store or whatever grows in your garden. I promise you'll be able to make it work!

TALL BOYS

A Tall Boy is any flower that has a really long stem. I use these flowers to create height and movement and to draw visual lines in arrangements. Whether used en masse or just as an accent, they keep the eye moving upward in an otherwise low, round arrangement.

ANTHURIUM

ALLIUM

DELPHINIUM

NERINE

POPPY

TULIP

SHOWSTOPPERS

These are large, often (but not always!) pricey blooms used to create focal points in your arrangement. Use them in a cluster to really draw in the eye or as a single large bloom to complement other smaller, daintier flowers.

GARDEN ROSE

PEONY

DAHLIA

PHALAENOPSIS ORCHID

TEXTURE HEAVY

Feathery grasses and textural florals add interest to your arrangements. These can create either a softening effect, like explosion grass, or a more structured feeling, as with oncidium.

CELOSIA

EXPLOSION GRASS

ONCIDIUM

LILAC

DRIED

People love dried florals because they're everlasting. While I don't specialize in all-dried arrangements, I like to use them as accent pieces in fresh arrangements. Naturally, dried florals are muted in color, as they're often bleached in the preservation process; however, you can find them dyed in an array of colors.

STYPHA

DRIED HYDRANGEA

DRIED PALM LEAF

ASPARAGUS FERN

FILLER

Filler refers to any stem that adds bulk and volume to an arrangement; it is also used to fill in any gaps or holes. Traditionally, low-cost greenery is used as filler, but I also love to use low-cost flowers.

CARNATION

MUMS

LISIANTHUS

ANTHURIUM LEAF

TROPICALS

I love tropicals for their hardy, long-lasting vase life and the bright array of colors they come in. I tend to always use at least one tropical stem in my work to add that little punch of fun and intrigue.

BANANA FLOWER

HELICONIA HANGING

PINCUSHION PROTEA

VANDA ORCHID

WEIRDOS

Weirdos add intrigue and mystery to arrangements, though they have a tendency to steal the show. They usually leave the recipient asking, "Is that even real?!" And that's what I love most about the Weirdos—they'll quickly turn arrangements into conversation starters.

DATE BERRIES

GLORIOSA LILY

LIPSTICK PODS

TORCH GINGER

II.
LET'S MAKE SOME ARRANGE-MENTS

Now that you have an understanding of the basics, let's get to the fun part: flowering! In the pages that follow, you'll find six different arrangement styles, each with three or four arrangements illustrating that style.

I wanted this section of the book to feel similar to a cookbook—a format most of us are familiar with. With that in mind, each arrangement is presented in the same way a recipe would be: It has a photo of the finished arrangement, a list of materials, a list of flowers you'll need, and step-by-step instructions with accompanying photos showing how I built each arrangement. The only difference is that we're working with flowers instead of food.

When following these recipes and recreating these arrangements, don't feel as if you have to follow each step to a T. I want you to use the recipes as a blueprint, but feel free to go off script and build your own version of each arrangement. Why? Well, because it's going to be nearly impossible for you to recreate an arrangement exactly as you see it in this book. Chances are you're reading this in another climate with access to entirely different flowers. Or maybe you live in a small town with only a small grocery store selection of flowers. So don't worry too much about finding the exact variety of flower or even the exact same type of vase.

Use the Flower Glossary to find swaps. For example, in the Reflexed Rose Explosion on page 81, I use roses and dahlias, both Showstoppers, as well as dyed explosion grass. If you can't find those two blooms, swap them for another Showstopper or two, such as peonies or mums, or another bloom with a similar fluffy, spherical shape, such as a carnation. If you can't find explosion grass, use troll grass or asparagus fern, both of which add a textured, fluffy aspect to your arrangement. I want you to experiment, riff, and create your own versions of each arrangement.

Since we're talking about choosing and sourcing flowers, I should mention that flowers are almost always sold in bunches, save for a few types of flowers sold by the stem (anthuriums, hydrangeas, tropicals). Most recipes in this book don't call for a full bunch, so if you're following these recipes, you'll almost always have leftover flowers. That's just part of the game when making flower arrangements. Feel free to incorporate those leftovers into your arrangement to make it larger and grander, or perhaps make a few small bud vase arrangements to complement your showpiece. There are even a few arrangements that I suggest making specifically when you have a bunch of leftover flowers.

Above all, I encourage you to not take any of this too seriously. I found my personal style by educating myself and seeing what other people were doing, but mostly by just playing around and going with the flow. Remember to have fun with it!

Before You Get Started

The supply lists include measurements for vases. These measurements always refer to the size of the vase opening.

When building arrangements, I consider there to be three planes: the foreground, the middle ground, and the background. My instructions refer to these different planes. To visualize this, imagine you're standing in front of the vase and staring down into the opening. The foreground consists of the front half of the vase opening, the middle ground refers to the middle of the vase opening, and the background refers to the back half of the vase opening.

Your flowers are going to move, and that's okay! As you build your arrangement and add more stems, you'll see that some flowers shift and wiggle their way out of the position you first put them in. Sometimes you'll like how the flower settles and moves; other times you'll struggle to get it back into that exact original spot. It's inevitable!

360 ARRANGEMENTS

NOTE

To make your life easier when creating 360 arrangements, use a lazy Susan! Placing your vase on a lazy Susan while building your arrangement will allow you to easily turn it so that you're giving every angle the love and attention it deserves.

A 360 arrangement is a very nontechnical term for arrangements meant to be viewed from all sides and angles. These styles of arrangements often have a rounded shape and sometimes lack a central focal point. Think about it this way: Whereas with forward-facing arrangements you can arrange all the flowers with only one angle in mind (the front angle, where the viewer is standing), with a 360 arrangement you have to make sure anyone standing anywhere nearby is going to have a nice view. Because of that, 360 arrangements tend to be a bit looser and less geometric. These types of arrangements work best for dinner tables, party tables, coffee tables—basically any situation where the arrangement isn't going to be placed up against a wall. A friendly word of caution: It's inevitable that you're going to like one side of the arrangement more than the other. It's natural, and it happens to me every single time. In those cases, I make sure to place my arrangement with that side facing what I imagine will be the most viewed angle.

A WHIMSICAL, FLOSSY CLOUD

Believe it or not, those are not feathers you're looking at; it's a type of dried grass! Most commonly sold in its natural color, a soft beige troll grass is a really fun dried material that can be dyed any color you'd like (see how to on page 66). Given that troll grass is heavy in texture, my favorite way to use it is by pairing it with only one or two varieties of tall stems to create a fun, whimsical arrangement that doesn't look too busy. Throughout the years, I've made many variations of this arrangement, and while it might look advanced, it's really not that complicated to build. I used tulips and daisies in this variation, but feel free to use any combination of troll grass and tall-stemmed flowers; any mix of the two will achieve a similar look. When creating this type of arrangement, make sure to create fullness at the base, using the troll grass, and then use the tall stems to create different planes of height. Let the natural curves of each tall stem create flow and movement in the arrangement.

A WHIMSICAL, FLOSSY CLOUD

6 bunches dried troll grass (see note)

8 stems tulips (see note)

8 stems daisies

4 in [10 cm] low bowl (see note)

Kenzan (see note)

Chicken wire

Clear floral tape

NOTES

Troll Grass → I buy my troll in its natural color and use Rit dye to dye it whatever color I need (see page 66). If you're not up for a dye job, many floral suppliers carry it in various colors, already dyed for you.

Tulips → Preferably French tulips, as their stems are longer, though regular tulips will work as well. I used light yellow tulips here, but you can use any color that complements the color of your troll grass. I also like pink tulips with orange troll, and purple tulips with green troll.

Low Bowl → I suggest keeping the opening of your bowl on the smaller side. Troll grass is thin and tends to allow the chicken wire and mechanics to peep through. The smaller the opening, the less there is to cover up. You'll still be able to create a fairly large arrangement; you just won't need a big vessel to do so.

Kenzan → If you want to create extra stability and really make sure those long stems stay in place, you can use a $2\frac{3}{4}$ in [7 cm] kenzan at the base of the vase, under the chicken wire, as I did for the arrangement pictured. This is totally optional, though! The chicken wire will still hold your stems in place just fine; you just might have to mess around with the stems a bit more to get them to stay in place.

STEPS

1. Prepare the bowl using a kenzan and the chicken wire method (page 26). Fill the bowl three-quarters full with room-temperature water.

2. Place the troll grass bunches throughout the whole arrangement until you've used about 75 percent of the troll grass you have available. Start thinking about creating a rounded structure using the troll grass: Place some bunches facing upward, some facing to the side, and even some facing downward. Don't worry about any chicken wire still being visible; you'll cover that up at the end. (Note: If you're lucky, your troll grass will be delivered to you already gathered into tiny individual 1 in [2.5 cm] bunches that make this part easy. If instead you received your troll grass as one big mass of tiny grass blades, use wire or tape to create small 1 in [2.5 cm] clusters like the ones you see me using.)

3. Place your tulip stems in the arrangement. Don't overthink this step! What's important is to space the tulips somewhat evenly throughout the arrangement, creating lines in different directions using the natural curves of the tulip stems. Cut some stems short and place them closer to the base of the arrangement; keep other stems extra long, allowing them to create really long lines. Make sure to add a few closer to the edge of the vase and allow them to curve downward toward the table.

4. Follow the tulips with the daisies, using them to fill any holes or gaps that you couldn't fill with the tulips.

5. Once you've inserted the tulips and daisies, use the remaining troll grass to fill in any remaining gaps or holes in the arrangement.

A WHIMSICAL, FLOSSY CLOUD

3

3

4

DYE YOUR OWN TROLL GRASS

I'm going to be honest: Buying your dried florals already dyed is the easiest thing to do, especially if you're just learning and experimenting with making your own arrangements. But sometimes it might be difficult to find the exact color you need; that's when knowing how to dye your own troll grass might come in handy. I use Rit brand liquid dye on my florals, as I love their color range, and using the dye is really simple. You're never going to get a super punchy, vibrant color using this method, but I do love the soft pastel hues it adds to troll grass. This can get a bit messy, so make sure you're doing this either outside or over a tarp. (Note: This dye method also works great with pampas grass!)

HOW TO DYE TROLL GRASS:

1. Fill a 1 gal [3.8 L] bucket about three-quarters full with room-temperature water.

2. Add an entire 8 oz [240 ml] bottle of dye to the water and mix. If you want a more saturated color, add two 8 oz [240 ml] bottles. Stir to ensure the dye is completely blended.

3. Submerge the troll grass in the dye bucket and let it sit for about 20 minutes.

4. Remove the troll grass from the bucket, being mindful that it's going to drip a bit. To reduce the mess, I like to move my wet troll grass into an empty bucket and let it drip-dry in there.

5. Use a blow dryer (yes, just your plain old hair dryer!) to dry the troll grass. I've found it's best to set the dryer on medium heat and aim it from the stem end toward the plumes. There will be a few minutes when you question whether the grass will ever look like it did before it got wet, but have patience; with some time it will dry and look like its former self!

HOW TO REFLEX FLOWERS

Reflexing is the practice of manually opening flowers. Reflexing flowers happens to be one of my favorite tricks to show people, because it's really easy to do and makes such a difference. Just look at those reflexed tulips in A Whimsical, Flossy Cloud (page 61)—they're just so fun!

In addition to tulips, roses can be reflexed as well. (Look at Reflexed Rose Explosion on page 81!) The trick is to use roses that have been out of the cooler for two to three days. It sounds counterintuitive, but this technique works better with roses that have started to naturally open on their own. Try this with fresh, just-out-of-the-flower-cooler roses, and you're bound to break a bunch of petals.

HOW TO REFLEX FLOWERS:

1. Hold the bloom firmly with one hand at the top of the stem, just under the flower base.

2. With the other hand, start softly inverting the petals, flipping each petal so it curves outward instead of inward. The best way to do this is to put your thumb at the base of the petal and use your index and middle fingers to gently pop the petal in the other direction. Do this gently enough, and you won't damage the petals.

3. If your flower has only one row of petals, like a tulip, work your way around all the petals until you have a much more opened flower. For flowers with multiple rows, like a rose, continue to invert a few rows of petals, then use your fingers to gently create space in the center of the rose.

SHE'S FLIRTY, SHE'S FUN

I have always loved the look of an invisible vase arrangement, as it really lets the flowers have their moment. Traditionally, invisible vase arrangements were made using floral foam, but it's the twenty-first century, and ignoring the negative impact of floral foam on the environment is very uncool. To achieve the same look without using floral foam, I use a very low, clear dish with chicken wire. You must be extra careful when moving your arrangement (the low dish allows water to spill more easily), but the effect is nearly identical.

I've found that the invisible vase look works best when you really fill the arrangement with a mass of fluffy flowers. If you use small, delicate flowers you'll find yourself having to use way too many to conceal the vase and the mechanics. When I think of full, fluffy arrangements, I automatically think of classical arrangements, much like the ones I imagine Marie Antoinette had placed around Versailles. Hers might have been a little too stuffy for my taste, so here's my take on a rococo-inspired arrangement using an invisible vase.

SHE'S FLIRTY,
SHE'S FUN

FLOWERS

5 stems hydrangea

3 stems delphinium

7 stems lisianthus (see note)

9 stems roses

1 stem allium

TOOLS

5 in [13 cm] clear Lomey designer dish (see note)

Chicken wire

Clear floral tape

NOTES

Lisianthus → Here I used a Japanese variety that is very fluffy and open. If you're using a smaller, less fluffy variety, you might need a few more stems.

Clear Lomey Designer Dish → You can find these at most floral supply stores and online (search for "designer dish"). Don't ask me why they're called designer dishes, as I truly have no idea, but they're almost always marketed to be used with floral foam. Look for ones with a higher side wall ($1\frac{1}{2}$ to 2 in [4 to 5 cm] tall) so that you can add a good amount of water. Given a choice of glass or plastic, choose glass, because the weight of the glass gives you a sturdier base. Plastic will work; just be extra mindful of weight distribution and take care when moving or transporting the arrangement.

STEPS

1. Prepare the dish using the chicken wire method (page 26). Scrunch the chicken wire so it creates a dome above the vase, essentially doubling the height of the designer dish. Fill the dish three-quarters full with room-temperature water.

2. To create a base, insert four hydrangea stems toward the front left and back left corners, angled in different directions.

3. Start adding height and a vertical line with two delphinium stems to the center right.

4. Add the lisianthus stems in the foreground, projecting outward and not too close to the base, creating visual interest and texture. Make sure you aren't clustering them together; leave room for the roses to live in between and behind them. Repeat this at the back of the arrangement as well.

5. Add one more delphinium pointing toward the opposite side of the first two delphiniums. Just make sure it's cut a little shorter than the other delphiniums, otherwise your arrangement might look like it has bunny ears!

6. Add the last hydrangea stem on the side opposite the first three, positioning it down low so it's sort of beneath the delphinium.

7. Fill any gaps in the arrangement using rose stems. This may lead to small clusters of roses; if that happens, that's okay! Just make sure to vary the distance of the roses from the core of the arrangement. They shouldn't all be right next to each other. Here, for example, I added one single stem of a rose at a much taller height than the others and reflexed it slightly. Repeat this at the rear of the arrangement.

8. Add the single allium stem, slightly off center, pointing in the direction opposite the first two delphiniums.

SHE'S FLIRTY, SHE'S FUN

2

3

4

5

6

7

8

TROPICAL(ISH)[2]

Remember how I said that 360 arrangements often lack
a central focal point? Well, there are a few exceptions, and
one of them is what I like to call mirrored arrangements.
In a mirrored arrangement, one side is a mirror image of
the other side. When I create these types of arrangements,
I'll normally put something large and flat, like a fan palm,
in the middle to divide the arrangement in half. In a way,
the palm gives the illusion of a divider, making it easy to
create two distinct sides. These types of arrangements
work especially well on long rectangular dinner tables.

TROPICAL(ISH)²

2 stems anthurium

2 stems delphinium

1 stem fan palm

2 or 3 stems fruiting date

8 stems lisianthus (see note)

2 stems oncidium orchid

One 5 in [13 cm] footed bowl (see note)

Chicken wire

Clear floral tape

Lisianthus → I used a Japanese variety here that is very fluffy and open. If you're using a smaller, less fluffy variety of lisianthus, you might need a few more stems.

Footed Bowl → If you don't have a footed bowl, a regular low bowl will work as well.

STEPS

1. Prepare the vase using the chicken wire method (page 26). Fill the vase three-quarters full with room-temperature water.

2. Insert one anthurium on the lower-right lip of the vase with the spadix pointing downward.

3. Add two delphiniums in the left middle ground of the vase, pointing to ten and eleven o'clock. Leave them both around the same height.

4. Add the fan palm in the right middle ground of the vase. Visually it should be behind the anthurium.

5. Add two fruiting date stems in the left foreground, just below the delphinium. You want these to be cascading downward and grazing the surface on which the vase sits.

6. Use four of the lisianthus to start filling in the left foreground of the vase, saving the other four for the other side of the arrangement.

7. Add one oncidium orchid stem on the right just between the anthurium and the fan palm. Let the orchid stem arc down to the right. If you're using a third fruiting date stem, add it beneath the orchid on the right.

8. Once one side of the arrangement starts taking shape and you really love how it's looking, start mirroring your actions on the other side of the palm leaf. Add the remaining anthurium, four lisianthus, and one orchid stem on the other side of the palm leaf so it looks the same on both sides. (You don't need to duplicate the palm leaf—since it's set vertically and will appear on both sides—or the delphinium, which is tall enough to be equally visible from both sides.)

TROPICAL(ISH)²

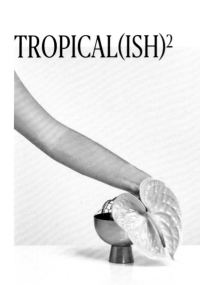

REFLEXED ROSE EXPLOSION

Roses get a lot of hate. I get it! We're so used to seeing the dozen red roses at the grocery store, all tightly closed up, wrapped in a bunch of plastic, looking like they have only about an hour of life left. I'm here to ask you to give them a second chance. This arrangement uses an easy little trick that's going to make you fall in love with roses again. We're reflexing! (See page 67.) Just as they'd open up if left on the bush, the act of reflexing finds you flipping open rose petals to create a full-blown rose. A reflexed rose takes up a lot of real estate in an arrangement, so I love to pair the big, dramatic blooms with a dainty, textured green or grass. In this arrangement, I paired Pink Floyd roses (one of the easiest roses to reflex) with burgundy-dyed explosion grass, and I added a few dahlias for fullness. The result is a sprawling, juxtaposed, and playful mix of big Showstopper flowers and delicate, texture-heavy explosion grass.

REFLEXED ROSE EXPLOSION

FLOWERS

1 bunch dyed explosion grass (see note)

9 stems standard roses, reflexed (see note)

4 stems small dahlias

TOOLS

5 in [13 cm] cylinder vase (see note)

Chicken wire

Clear floral tape

NOTES

Explosion Grass → If you can't find dyed explosion grass, you can spray-paint your own using Design Master spray paint, made just for fresh flowers.

Roses → Some varieties of roses are easier to reflex. I find the Pink Floyd variety to be one of the easiest. Follow the steps on page 67 to reflex almost any standard rose.

Cylinder Vase → This arrangement uses a vase with a slight shape, but any cylindrical vase will work.

STEPS

1. Prepare the vase using the chicken wire method (page 26). Fill the bowl three-quarters full with room-temperature water.

2. Place a few stems of explosion grass going in opposite directions so you can start with an idea of how widely the grass will spread.

3. Place a single rose slightly off-center, with the bloom resting on the lip of the vase. Place one rose to the left of the central rose and another to the right. You want them at different heights, angled away from the central rose and each other.

4. Add two more roses, one sharply angled to the left, the other a little less sharply angled to the right. The roses should feel a little chaotic, in that they're all pointing in different directions. You're going to fill in that space with more explosion grass.

5. Notice you now have a gap in the low center of the vase. Fill that in with the rest of the roses. Cut them to different lengths and make sure to leave some room in between them so they aren't crowded.

6. Use the dahlias to fill in any remaining gaps toward the center of the arrangement. In the end, you want open space on the outer edges of the arrangement but not so much in the middle.

7. Add the remaining explosion grass until you feel you have the fullness and fluffiness you're looking for.

2

3

REFLEXED ROSE EXPLOSION

4

JUICY SUNBURST

The majority of my work tends to be airy, loose, and stemmy.
There's very rarely a tight ball of flowers at the core of the
arrangement. It's probably just my way of trying to rebel against
the more traditional, tight-looking arrangements we're so used
to seeing in the floral world. Still, sometimes a small table filled
with candles and other decor calls for something a little more
compact. When I *do* make tighter arrangements, I always make
sure to have a few cascading stems as well as a few Tall Boys
jutting out. Because of this, these arrangements tend to be more
vertical. This one, which I'm calling Juicy Sunburst thanks to all
those yummy, colorful blooms, is the perfect example of that: an
arrangement that feels full and fun without taking up too much
real estate.

JUICY SUNBURST

FLOWERS

6 stems garden roses
4 stems dahlias
2 stems anthurium
1 stem vanda orchid
3 stems carnations
1 stem celosia
2 stems oncidium orchid
1 stem phalaenopsis orchid

TOOLS

6 in [15 cm] low bowl
Chicken wire
Clear floral tape

STEPS

1. Prepare the bowl using the chicken wire method and clear tape (page 26). Fill the bowl three-quarters full with room-temperature water.

2. Place three garden roses at the lip of the bowl to start building a base. Counter that by placing two dahlias above the garden roses— one high up on the right, pointing to one o'clock, and one sitting just above the roses on the left. Since this is a 360 arrangement, make sure to repeat these steps on the opposite side of the arrangement.

3. Continue building the height of the arrangement, keeping all of the flowers clustered pretty closely together. I added a few more dahlias and roses just above the initial ones I placed at the lip of the bowl.

4. Add one anthurium, which will be one of the tallest points of your arrangement. Since my anthurium curved to the left, I played with that attribute and placed it leaning toward eleven o'clock. My other anthurium had the same orientation, so I placed it low, just in front of the first anthurium.

5. Add the vanda orchid, leaning it slightly to the right, at the center of your arrangement. This will help keep your arrangement feeling more vertical rather than sprawling and horizontal. I love using vanda orchids for 360 arrangements because, unlike other orchids, they have blooms on both sides of their stems. I added a carnation stem and the celosia stem to fill in holes.

6. Add two oncidium orchid stems to the right, counteracting the left lean of the tall anthurium. This adds a softer touch and a bit more verticality without asking too much of your attention (as a really bold bloom would).

7. Finish your arrangement by placing the phalaenopsis stem cascading downward, toward the side of the arrangement. Fill in any holes with extra carnations, roses, or dahlias.

6

7

7

FORWARD-FACING ARRANGEMENTS

To put it simply, forward-facing arrangements are meant to be viewed from one side only. The person making the arrangement focuses all the flowers on one side of the arrangement, leaving the other side either bare or with just a minimal amount of stems and foliage.

Most of my favorite arrangements are forward facing, mainly because I love how the absence of flowers in the background allows for the forward-facing flowers in the foreground to catch the viewer's attention without any visual noise behind them. These qualities also make forward-facing arrangements some of the easiest to photograph, given how graphic and bold they can look. These types of arrangements work best in entryways or any situation where your arrangement will be placed against a wall.

A TROPICAL DELIGHT

This is an arrangement I come back to repeatedly, as it's so
chic and minimal—it really pops! It requires only two types of
flowers—anthuriums and orchids—but it still feels special, even
monumental. I particularly love to use phalaenopsis orchids in this
arrangement for the cascading effect they create over the front of
the vase. Given that all the anthuriums face forward, this is truly
one of those arrangements that has nothing going for it on the
other side, so make sure to tuck this baby up against a wall!

A TROPICAL DELIGHT

FLOWERS

7 stems anthurium (see note)
1 stem phalaenopsis orchid (see note)

TOOLS

4 in [10 cm] low bowl (see note)
Kenzan

NOTES

Anthurium → While you can use just one color of anthurium, I like to use two—one in the dominant color (in this example, the green) and another in a complementary color (the burnt orange).

Phalaenopsis → Whenever I've made this arrangement, I've always used a phalaenopsis stem that is just a few shades lighter than one of the anthurium colors. Here, I love how this light orange stem echoes the deep orange of the anthuriums.

Low Bowl → While this arrangement does have some spread, there are only eight stems being inserted into it, so the opening can be fairly small. Keep in mind that the phalaenopsis has some weight, so you want to use a bowl that's heavy enough to anchor the arrangement. Here I used a ceramic bowl.

ANTHURIUM ORIENTATIONS

■ You'll notice that most anthuriums have a natural lean, pointing to the right or the left or sometimes directly upward. It's important to acknowledge the orientation of each anthurium and place it accordingly. For example, in this arrangement, I made sure to use anthuriums that were oriented to the left for the bottom left corner. If I had used an anthurium pointing to the right, I would not have gotten the fanned-out look I was going for.

PHALAENOPSIS TRICK

■ Cut phalaenopsis stems are normally sold by the box, so to use just one stem, you normally have to buy at least ten, which will cost you a pretty penny. A good hack that I use when I need just one stem is to buy a potted orchid plant and cut the stem myself. The cost of the plant is almost always the same as a single stem, and I also get a cute plant out of it! Win–win.

STEPS

1. Prepare the bowl using a kenzan. Fill the bowl three-quarters full with room-temperature water.

2. Place a single anthurium, with the stem kept long, pointing toward one o'clock. Insert the stem in the middle of the kenzan to leave room for stems that will be inserted in the foreground.

3. Place another anthurium to the left of the vase, low and close to the lip of the vase. You'll want to orient this anthurium in the opposite direction of the first.

4. Insert a third and fourth anthurium: one just behind but slightly higher, pointing toward eleven o'clock, and the other situated slightly in front of the low one, also pointing toward eleven o'clock.

5. Insert the phalaenopsis stem slightly to the right of center and in the front of the chicken wire and kenzan so the blooms cascade forward over the front of the bowl.

6. Take one of the complementary-colored anthuriums, cut it short, and place it in the center of the arrangement, just behind the phalaenopsis stem. Its spadix should point downward; depending on the orientation of your anthurium, this might mean the end of the stem doesn't reach the water in the vase. If this is the case, use a water tube as I did here.

7. Place the second complementary-colored anthurium just behind the phalaenopsis at medium height and pointing toward two o'clock. Finish off with one extra-long anthurium set at a much higher plane, pointing toward eleven o'clock.

A TROPICAL DELIGHT

5

4

6

7

ALL ABOUT ALLIUMS

Alliums are up there among my all-time favorite flowers.
I mean, what other flower looks like a perfectly purple fluffy
ball? Though they come in a few different sizes and varieties,
my favorite is the *Allium gigantum* species—they're so large,
round, and playful looking. Since I consider these to be a total
showstopper (an instance where a flower can be both a Tall Boy
and a Showstopper!), I love to pair them with just one other
equally stunning flower to create what I usually refer to as a big
mound of flowers. For this particular arrangement, I chose these
really beautiful pincushion proteas to complement the alliums,
but any flower with a large spherical bloom will work here.

ALL ABOUT ALLIUMS

10 stems allium (see note)
8 stems pincushion proteas

6 in [15 cm] low bowl (see note)
Chicken wire
Clear floral tape
2 water tubes

~~~~~~

Allium → Any large variety of allium will work.

Low Bowl → This arrangement can get a little heavy, so make sure you choose a bowl with some weight to it. If not, be mindful of weight distribution when placing your stems!

STEPS

1. Prepare your bowl using the chicken wire method (page 26). Fill the bowl three-quarters full with room-temperature water.

2. Start by cutting one allium short and placing it in the low center foreground of the bowl. Create an asymmetrical V formation by adding three more alliums, one of middling height leaning off to the right of the first allium, and two leaning off to the left of the first allium. Of the two on the left, one stem should be very tall, and the other should be around the same height as the allium leaning to the right.

3. Add one pincushion protea to the lower right side of your arrangement so you can start to get an idea of the size of the pincushion in relation to the alliums. This pincushion protea should be cut fairly short and sit just slightly above the lip of the bowl.

4. Add another tall allium to the right of center, and start filling the gaps closest to the bowl with pincushion proteas and alliums.

5. Place a single allium, cut short, on the surface in front and to the right of the bowl. Use a water tube on the stem so this flower is receiving water.

6. Place another allium, cut short, on the surface in front of the bowl, this time on the left side, again providing a water tube. The idea is to cover some of the bowl so the arrangement feels more integrated with the surface it's resting on.

7. Use the remaining blooms to fill in space upward and outward. You want to create what appears like a mound of just blooms, with few stems showing.

2

2

2

3

4

5

7

PINK GINGER PUNCH

Song of India is a common houseplant, and its naturally curving, two-toned leaves are some of my favorites to work with. In this arrangement, the leaves act like fingers, creating long lines that draw the eye upward and outward. At the center, the ginger creates a focal point with its punchy pink color and slight curves. The bunch of green grapes cascading downward and just slightly grazing the surface below the vase adds an unexpected touch of whimsy that also happens to be edible! Because this arrangement has quite a lot going on in terms of texture, I stuck to a two-tone color palette of greens and pinks, one of my favorite color combinations.

PINK GINGER PUNCH

FLOWERS

4 stems song of India (three kept very long, one cut fairly short)

5 stems astilbe

6 stems daisies

3 stems ginger

2 large bunches of grapes

TOOLS

5 in [13 cm] cylinder vase (see note)

Chicken wire

Clear floral tape

1 water tube

NOTE

Cylinder Vase → I wanted to emphasize the cascading effect of the grapes, so I used a footed vase to add some height.

STEPS

1. Prepare the vase using the chicken wire method (page 26). Fill three-quarters full with room-temperature water.

2. Place three song of India stems on the right-hand side of the arrangement. To create a fanning effect, place one pointing upward, one pointing to about three o'clock, and the third pointing downward toward five o'clock. The stem pointing to five o'clock may need a water tube if the stem ends aren't submerged in the water. A water tube will ensure that the flowers are getting hydrated while also pointing downward.

3. Start filling in the right side of the arrangement with the astilbe stems. You want to use these to fill in the negative space that isn't being covered by the song of India, so don't make them too tall! In this arrangement they're acting as filler, so they should sit fairly close to the base of the vase.

4. So you can start visually balancing the arrangement, add three daisy stems on the left pointing upward and outward to the left. You'll add the rest later, once you get a sense of how much space is left in the chicken wire after adding the big, chunky ginger stems.

5. Add the three ginger stems in the center and slightly off to the left. These are acting as focal flowers in this arrangement, so keep them low and close to the opening of the vase. Ginger tends to have a natural curve; work with these curves to create another fanning effect.

6. Add the first bunch of grapes just behind the ginger and cascading down to the left. Don't worry about the stem of the grape touching the water; it won't make a difference in the lifespan of the grapes.

7. Place the second bunch of grapes to rest directly on top of the chicken wire. You want the grapes to cover any chicken wire that remains visible in the center of the arrangement. Using your hands, guide the grapes to do this while also making sure the grapes appear to be spilling out of the arrangement.

8. Finish off the left side of the arrangement with the remaining daisy stems, with some stems longer and some shorter.

9. If your arrangement is like mine, you might still have a gap of exposed chicken wire on the back left-hand side of the arrangement where the daisies are situated. If that's the case, use a very short stem of song of India to cover it up.

PINK GINGER PUNCH

6

7

8

TALL ARRANGEMENTS

NOTE

The height of the flowers or plant material should be at least the same height as or taller than the vase holding them. For example, in Fountain of Fireworks (page 121), the single oncidium stem is taller than the height of the vase, which creates a balanced look. Short flowers in a very tall vase look off.

I have a love-hate relationship with tall arrangements. On the one hand, I love anything in this life that is grand and over-the-top; on the other hand, a good tall arrangement can be hard to make! First, you have to find the right vase. It can be tricky to find a nice-looking tall vase that isn't crazy expensive. You also have to find the right flowers, leaves, and branches with enough size and oomph, because smaller, daintier options won't work here. Think big, graphic, bold. That's why a lot of my tall arrangements have either branches or large tropical leaves, both of which take up lots of space. Tall and vertically oriented arrangements work great when set on the floor or on any kind of side table or surface where you need some height. I like to display them on the floor next to my entryway table and my entertainment console.

ON BIG ISLAND TIME

Using large, graphic tropical leaves is one of the easiest ways to make big arrangements. With these larger-than-life-stems, you don't need many to make something grand and striking. I made this arrangement using only eight stems, and it was almost as tall as I am. Taking advantage of the natural curves and orientations of the leaves, this arrangement is an explosion of tropical greens, funky bromeliad flowers, and everyone's favorite Weirdo, a hanging heliconia!

ON BIG ISLAND TIME

1 banana leaf

2 firework bromeliad flowers

1 dried *Livistona* palm (see note)

1 hanging heliconia

2 palmetto fans

1 caladium leaf

1 anthurium leaf

TOOLS

Tall vase with a
4½ in [11 cm] opening (see note)

Chicken wire

Clear floral tape

Leaf shine (see note)

NOTES

Livistona → *Livistona* palm leaves tend to dry however they want. Some dry upright and like a big fan; others dry curled. Look for one that resembles a wave. If you're drying your own, dry it standing up (not flat) to encourage it to take on a wave-like shape.

Tall Vase → Any height will work here, but the taller the better. Make sure the height of the vase isn't taller than your tallest leaf (in this case, the banana leaf); otherwise, the proportions will feel off.

Leaf Shine → Florists often spray their tropical leaves with a product called leaf shine for a super-glossy sheen. You definitely don't need to do this, but it does add an extra bit of glam.

STEPS

1. Prepare the vase using the chicken wire method (page 26). With a tall vase, make sure to cluster the chicken wire close to the vase opening. Since these larger tropical leaves tend to be a bit heavier, I try to make my ball pretty tight. But not too tight! You want the thick stems to be able to fit into the nooks and crannies of the chicken wire. Fill the vase three-quarters full with room-temperature water.

2. Add the banana leaf toward the back of the vase, leaning slightly to the left.

3. Add two bromeliad flowers toward the back of the vase, leaning slightly to the right.

4. Place the dried palm leaf toward the right of the arrangement, sitting just at the lip of the vase.

5. Place the heliconia stem toward the left of the arrangement. You want the hanging part to appear as if it's just hanging off the lip of the vase. Cut off any remaining stem that projects upward from the hanging part.

6. Place a palmetto fan just behind the heliconia, oriented to the left, and the other behind the bromeliad flowers, oriented upward. In terms of spacing, the banana leaf and palmetto fans should be in the background, and the bromeliad flowers, palm leaf, and heliconia in the foreground.

7. Add the caladium leaf in the foreground, to the left of the dried palm.

8. Finish off with a single glossy anthurium leaf on the right-hand side, pointing downward.

6

7

8

FOUNTAIN OF FIREWORKS

When creating tall arrangements, it's sometimes inevitable that the vase is going to show. Unlike with other types of arrangements, where you can conceal the vase or make it less noticeable, with tall arrangements you have to work with the vase to make it feel integrated with the flowers.

This style of arrangement is all about the vase. Here, I used a beautiful vintage Haeger vase that has a lot of personality on its own. For that reason, I didn't want to make the arrangement overly complicated or busy; instead I used just two varietals and focused on matching the movement of the flowers with the shape and flow of the vase. If you don't just happen to have a vintage Haeger vase lying around (there are always some for sale on Etsy and eBay), look for alternatives with interesting shapes and designs so the vase is as visually appealing as the arrangement it holds. To achieve the fanning effect with the stems, look for a vase with a cavity taller than it is wide and narrower at its base than at its opening.

FOUNTAIN OF FIREWORKS

FLOWERS

8 stems upright amaranth (see note)

7 stems oncidium orchid

TOOL

Tall vase

NOTES

Amaranth → I used a burnt-orange variety in this arrangement, but green upright amaranth would look beautiful as well. Just make sure you're getting the right variety of amaranth—that is, an upright variety and not a hanging one.

Mechanics → I did not use any mechanics here, given the small opening of the vase. Instead, I used the separate chambers of the vase to hold the flowers in place.

STEPS

1. Fill the vase three-quarters full with room-temperature water.

2. Begin creating a fanning effect with the amaranth on the right side of the vase. I used five amaranth stems, each of slightly different heights.

3. Using three more amaranth stems, create the same effect on the left side. Cut these stems shorter so the fan doesn't drape as far, to create an asymmetrical look.

4. In the gap left in the middle, fill in using all the oncidium stems, cut at different lengths. You want the oncidium stems to be taller than the amaranth on the left but almost the same height as the amaranth on the right. The oncidium stems should round out the curved line you're creating with the tops of the flowers: Some oncidium stems should curve to the left, some should be oriented more upward, and a few should point to the right, creating a fairly even arc.

5. Finish by placing one last oncidium stem, cut very long, in the center of the arrangement so it curves upward and slightly to the right.

FOUNTAIN OF FIREWORKS

5

5

SWINGING AMARANTH

Early spring tends to be an exciting time for florists because
everything starts blooming after a long, cold winter. Also
because: flowering branches! For just a short time, the flower
markets become filled with flowering branches of all kinds:
cherry blossoms, magnolia, and quince, just to name a few.
And since the blooming period is so short, you know that I'm
going to be using them in just about everything for those few
weeks. The one thing I will say about flowering branches is that
they sometimes feel a little too serious, with their tall, towering
branches and small, delicate flowers. In this arrangement, we
add a twist that makes the configuration of branches just a
little bit more fun and funky!

SWINGING AMARANTH

FLOWERS

3 stems quince (see note)

6 stems hanging amaranth

TOOLS

Tall vase, preferably with a unique shape for this simpler arrangement

NOTES

Quince → When it comes to flowering branches, their structures can be really wonky! At first, you might find that annoying. (I want the branch to lean this way; why is it leaning the other way?) The best advice I can give is to just lean into it. Take a look at your branch, figure out where the natural curve is, and use that to your advantage. As an example, if your branch has a left-leaning curve to it, use it on the left side of your arrangement.

Long branches usually have several little branches jutting off from them. Sometimes a little branch gets in the way of the harmony and balance of your arrangement. If that's the case, just chop off the little branch! I promise no one will notice it's missing.

Mechanics → Since this is a fairly narrow vase, with a minimal number of branches, I made this arrangement without any mechanics. If you're not feeling confident enough to go au naturel, the chicken wire method would work best here.

STEPS

1. Fill the vase three-quarters full with room-temperature water.

2. Add the first branch of quince so it's leaning to the left.

3. Add the second stem leaning to the right. (You'll see that one pesky little branch was in the way, so I chopped it off.)

4. Add the third branch in the middle of the arrangement. (My branch had a right-leaning curve to it, so it feels a little off-center, with a lean toward the right.)

5. Insert the amaranth stems into the vase and hang the strands from the flowering branches. Drape some more dramatically than others.

SWINGING AMARANTH

BUD VASES + TINY ARRANGEMENTS

When I first started working with florals, I avoided bud vases. The idea of adding two to three stems to a tiny vase felt too simplistic and lacking any sort of character. Anybody could put together a small cluster of bud vases and call it a day—I was a very serious florist, and I wanted to be creating very serious arrangements!

Over the years, I've gotten over that thinking, and my attitude toward bud vases has shifted to one of loving and appreciating them, especially for their range. See, what I failed to notice back in the day is that there are so many ways to elevate and modernize a simple cluster of bud vases. Like in Good Things Come in Threes (page 143), where a cluster of three small to medium vases comes together with just a few stems to create a simple arrangement of flowers that resemble a modern version of a still life painting. Or how Anything Can Be a Vase Mélange (page 149) proves that just about anything in your home can become a bud vase—even champagne coupes and candlestick holders! So maybe you were once like me and wrote off bud vases as basic and boring. If so, I hope that the arrangements that follow change your mind and show you how to appreciate the very thing we once discounted—their simplicity!

ANATOMY OF
A BUD VASE

If we're going to do bud vases, let's do them right! When making
bud vase arrangements, I follow a few simple rules so that they
feel dynamic, varied, and well balanced. Instead of just throwing
in a bunch of stems at random lengths, I try to be intentional
about my placement and flower selection to create a bud vase
that stands out. Using different stems, I essentially create three
different levels: a bottom level with the blooms resting on the lip
of the vase, a middle level that fills the middle-ground space, and
a top level with one or two single blooms soaring over the rest of
the florals.

ANATOMY OF
A BUD VASE

1 stem celosia
1 stem rattlesnake calathea
1 stem garden rose
1 stem gloriosa lily
1 stem oncidium orchid
1 stem dahlia

TOOLS

1 bud vase
Chicken wire (optional; see note)

NOTE

Chicken Wire → Depending on the size
and style of bud vase you're using, you
might find that putting a small tube of
chicken wire in the vase will help to keep
stems in place. If that's the case, prep
your vase with chicken wire and skip
the tape.

STEPS

1. Prepare the vase by using the chicken wire method (page 26) if applicable. Fill the vase three-quarters full with room-temperature water.

2. Start by placing the large focal bloom at the lip of your vase. In this case, I'm using a celosia stem. I prefer my bud vases to appear bottom heavy rather than having large focal blooms high up.

3. Add the rattlesnake calathea to the right of the celiosa. Though bud vases tend to look more vertical, I still like for them to have some spread.

4. Next, at medium height, add the garden rose.

5. Start building up your height by adding the gloriosa stem to your vase. I love using gloriosa in bud vases because of how flirty and whimsical-looking they tend to be. Add the oncidium stem for height as well.

6. Finish your bud vase by filling in your medium height: Add a single dahlia in the center.

5

5

6

6

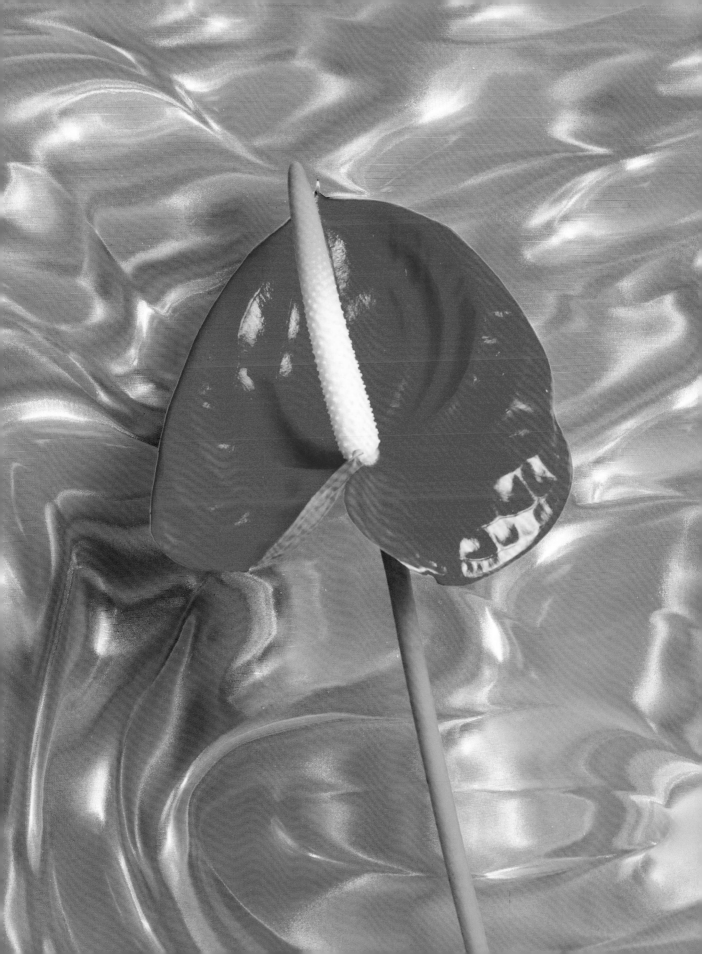

BEJEWEL YOUR FLOWERS

Using Gorilla Glue, attach craft jewels like gemstones and pearls to your flowers. I tend to do this with heartier flowers like anthuriums and orchids, as their petals can support the weight of the rhinestones.

GOOD THINGS COME
IN THREES

Okay, you'll have to forgive me—I know these aren't technically
bud vases. They're a little bigger than that. The vases pictured
are small to medium, with a 2½ to 4½ in [6 to 11 cm] opening.
Generally speaking, bud vases are shorter and smaller than that,
usually with a ½ to 2 in [13 mm to 5 cm] opening. But the point
is, not every cluster of bud vases has to be made using tiny vases,
and not every larger-opening vase has to be stuffed to the brim
with flowers. On the contrary, there's something kind of chic
about grouping three small to medium vases with just a few
stems in each. Like in this cluster, where I chose three vases
of different materials, heights, and colors that, when displayed
together, still feel harmonious. I used no more than four stems per
vase to create a fun, modern collection of flowers that skates the
line between a full-size arrangement and several tiny bud vases.

GOOD THINGS COME
IN THREES

FLOWERS

4 reflexed roses
2 stems peony
2 stems anthurium (see note)
1 stem phalaenopsis orchid
1 stem nerine

TOOLS

Three vases in three different heights
and colors—extra points if you use
three different materials too!
Chicken wire
Clear floral tape

NOTE

Anthurium → I used two different colors
of anthuriums here, but you could use a
single color.

STEPS

1. Prepare your vases using the chicken wire method (page 26). Fill the vases three-quarters full with room-temperature water. Arrange the vases in a triangular shape, with the shortest and medium ones in the foreground and the tallest in the back.

2. Fill the back vase with four roses. This will be the highest point of your arrangement, so feel free to really give those rose stems some length!

3. Add one peony in the front center of the shortest vase. This large focal bloom will act as a visual anchor. Add an anthurium to the same vase, facing to the right.

4. Add the second peony on the left side of the medium vase to act as a twin to the other peony.

5. Add the long phalaenopsis stem on the left side of the shortest vase and arrange it so the blooms are cascading toward the viewer. Add the other anthurium to the medium vase, just below and to the right of the peony, and orient it so the spadix is pointing to the right.

6. Add the nerine to the center of the shortest vase. Keep some height and let it fill any visual gap you might still see in the arrangement.

1

2

3

4

ANYTHING CAN BE
A VASE MÉLANGE

The last thing I want you to take away from this book is that you
need to go out and buy a bunch of tools, vases, and equipment to
realize your flower dreams. On the contrary, I want you to walk
away feeling like you already have most of what you need, and it's
just about changing the way you look at flower arranging. This
arrangement (or many arrangements!) is the perfect illustration.
For this mélange, I gathered all the different types of "bud
vases" I had in my house and then some. I collected champagne
coupes, candlesticks, and regular water glasses and grouped
them all together to create a mass of tiny arrangements. I can see
this conglomeration of glassware and flowers tripping merrily
down the center of a dinner table. Or maybe just on display on a
credenza or entryway table. Either way, the mix of flowers and
colored glass feels fun and random in the best possible way. The
key to this one is: Don't overthink it!

ANYTHING CAN BE A VASE MÉLANGE

FLOWERS

Here's a suggested mix of flowers that mimics what I used (see note):

Phalaenopsis orchid, for cascading effect

Allium, for large focal flower

Reflexed rose, for large focal flower

Dyed asparagus fern, for texture

Carnation, for a frilly bloom

Ranunculus, to create a dainty height element

Lotus pods, for a graphic moment

Gloriosa lily, for sprawling blooms that create lines

TOOLS

Here's a suggested mix of bud vases that mimics what I used:

Water glasses, especially ones with colored or textured/cut glass

Coupe glasses

Vintage cocktail glasses

Carafes

Wine bottles

Clean empty jars

Colorful ceramic mugs

Candlesticks with bud vase inserts
I love to use the ones from Base Vase

Votive holders and old candles
with wax removed

Actual bud vases!

NOTE

For this style of arrangement, you can use any assortment of leftover flowers. In this instance, I used the surplus plant material from a client order and simply gathered it together. And it works! If you're not going to use leftovers, then I suggest buying a variety of flowers of different heights, colors, and sizes to create a nice visual range.

STEPS

1. Fill all the vessels about three-quarters full with room-temperature water.

2. Spread out all the vessels on a work surface. Arrange them in a variety of heights and colors throughout, not spaced too perfectly. You want some to feel close to each other and others to feel more disconnected. Don't overthink this step; you can always rework it once the blooms are in their vessels.

3. Start adding blooms to the vessels: Put a single bloom in some, and more than one bloom in others. Take a step back every once in a while and take stock of how it's looking.

4. Once you've added all the flowers, ask yourself: Are there flowers at different heights throughout the mass? Are the flowers pointing in different directions? Are some flowers oriented toward the viewer and some situated away? If the answer to all is yes, then you're done! If not, keep playing with them until you're satisfied.

ANYTHING CAN BE A VASE MÉLANGE

PARTY-TIME FLOWERS

Back in my twenties, when I was still living in New York, I was always throwing a party. Even though I lived in the tiniest apartment, I was constantly looking for any reason to gather my friends, set the table, and create a makeshift dance floor in my living room. Now, a couple years later, I'm just a tiny bit older but somehow a lot more tired. Maybe it's all the labor involved with being a florist, or maybe it's the Miami heat making me lethargic. But I find myself hosting a lot less these days, which is kind of sad, given all the party floral ideas I've come up with through the years. Lucky for you, I've lived out three of my favorite party-time floral ideas in the pages of this book, so you can recreate them should you be up for throwing your own fête. How fun would it be to throw a dinner party and run a labyrinth of moss and flowers down the dinner table like on page 163? Or to host a funky, over-the-top dinner party with a colorful dessert table like on page 169? However and whatever you or I choose to celebrate, I think we can agree that flowers are always best enjoyed with company, so pull out the good china (does anyone still have "good china"?) and let's party!

CARNATIONS + CANDLES

This is the only time in this book when I'm going to tell you it's okay to display your flowers out of water. I'm making this exception because carnations tend to be very hardy and can go a few hours without water.

The first time I made this arrangement, I simply created it for myself and posted a photo to Instagram, not thinking many people would like it. Carnations have always been polarizing—many people associate them with cheap, dated bouquets—so I figured the post wouldn't be that popular. But it ended up getting a lot of likes! I still come across that very image on Pinterest frequently, so I think I was onto something.

I think what's most appealing about this look is that you can create a long labyrinth of candles and flowers for fairly cheap given the low cost of carnations. I envision this arrangement living on a dinner table, either in a lengthy, garland-like configuration on a rectangular table or in a circular mass on a round dinner table. Here, I made this arrangement on the simpler side; however, you can easily make it longer, even spanning the entire length of a table. Just multiply the materials and flowers needed by the amount of feet (or meters) you need to cover.

CARNATIONS + CANDLES

33 carnations (see note)

One 2½ in [6 cm] short, stout vase
Chicken wire
Clear floral tape
3 candlesticks and accompanying
taper candles (see note)
7 kenzans (see note)
Floral putty

Carnations → I used an equal mix of
carnations in three different colors that
complemented each other.

Candles → Any color candles work, but I
love the idea of using candles in the same
color as one of the three carnations.

Kenzans → I used six 2 in [5 cm] kenzans
and one $2\frac{1}{2}$ in [6 cm] kenzan.

STEPS

1. Prepare the vase using the chicken wire method (page 26). Fill it three-quarters full with room-temperature water. Situate the vase in the middle of the space and arrange the candles and kenzans around it in a configuration that feels random but still close.

2. Once you have a configuration you like, affix the kenzans to the table surface using a small amount of floral putty (enough to secure it but not so much that it's visible).

3. Start adding the carnations to the kenzans and vase. You want some carnations to be lying directly on the surface, some to be inserted into the kenzans (all at different heights), and some in the vase. As you add, you'll most likely want to readjust previous placements, which is totally normal! Sometimes you notice that you like/hate a placement only after you've added other things around it.

4. Once you're happy with your configuration and you're ready to party, light the candles!

WILD + MOSSY MOUNDS
FOR A DINNER TABLE

To say I'm obsessed with this arrangement would be an
understatement. It has everything I love: bright tropical flowers,
deep green mossy hues, and a really unexpected presentation.
Believe it or not, all the flowers and greenery in this arrangement
have a water source. You could never tell just by looking at it, but
there are three low bowls under all that moss, supporting most
of the flowers. To make it appear as if the arrangement was just
growing out of the table, I covered all the vases with moss and
vines. The result is a wild mix of flowers and greens that makes a
perfect dinner party arrangement. This is so easy to execute that
while I want to say you should save this for a special occasion,
given how striking it is, go ahead and flex your flowering skills
and make this for any festive affair.

WILD + MOSSY MOUNDS FOR A DINNER TABLE

FLOWERS

1 stem vanda orchid

1 stem phalaenopsis orchid

3 pincushion proteas

5 lotus pods

2 anthurium leaves

3 grevillea

3 stems anthurium

3 stems oncidium orchid

4 rattlesnake calatheas

5 stems celosia

3 vines, long and tendriled, any kind

NOTES

Flowers → Most of the flowers I used here are sold by the stem. Still, given the wide array of varieties, you could easily create this arrangement using leftover flowers (plus moss and vines).

Paper or Bubble Wrap → Though not necessary, you can use either material to support the moss and prop up one or two of the vases to create varying heights throughout the arrangement. Here I recycled a brown paper bag.

Moss → Sheet moss is usually sold by the box. I used the fresh variety for this, but preserved sheet moss will work just as well. If you're using fresh moss and plan to display this arrangement for several days, keep the moss moist and hydrated by spritzing it with water daily.

3 low bowl vases: 4¾ in [12 cm]; 2¾ in [7 cm], footed; 5½ in [14 cm]

Chicken wire
Clear floral tape
Paper or bubble wrap (optional; see note)
1 box of sheet moss (see note)
Water tubes

STEPS

1. Prepare the three bowls using the chicken wire method (page 26). Fill three-quarters full with room-temperature water. Cluster the bowls together about 3 in [7.5 cm] apart.

2. Crumple up pieces of construction paper (newspaper or bubble wrap would work too) and create mounds about 6 in [15 cm] high interspersed among the bowls. Start covering these mounds with clusters of moss. Once you've covered most of the paper with moss, the bowls will still be visible, and that's okay! You'll cover those soon with flowers and more moss.

3. Start adding flowers to the bowls, with some stems reaching up high and some lower, close to the lip of the bowl. You can also insert some florals directly into the moss; just use a water tube to provide water to those

blooms, and nestle the tubes into the moss so they're hidden. When thinking about the placement of your flowers, consider what attribute each flower brings to the setting and accentuate those qualities. For example, lotus pods have a long, sometimes curvy stem; for that reason, I used that stem to create a long line in the arrangement. Broad anthurium leaves take up a lot of space, so I used them to cover up large pieces of chicken wire. I balanced out the bold phalaenopsis orchids on the lower left by placing the airy, textural oncidium orchids on the upper right.

4. Once you've added a good bunch of flowers and the bowls are starting to be less visible, you can use the rest of the moss to cover up any remaining holes. It's really as simple as placing the moss directly on the chicken wire in the bowls.

WILD + MOSSY MOUNDS

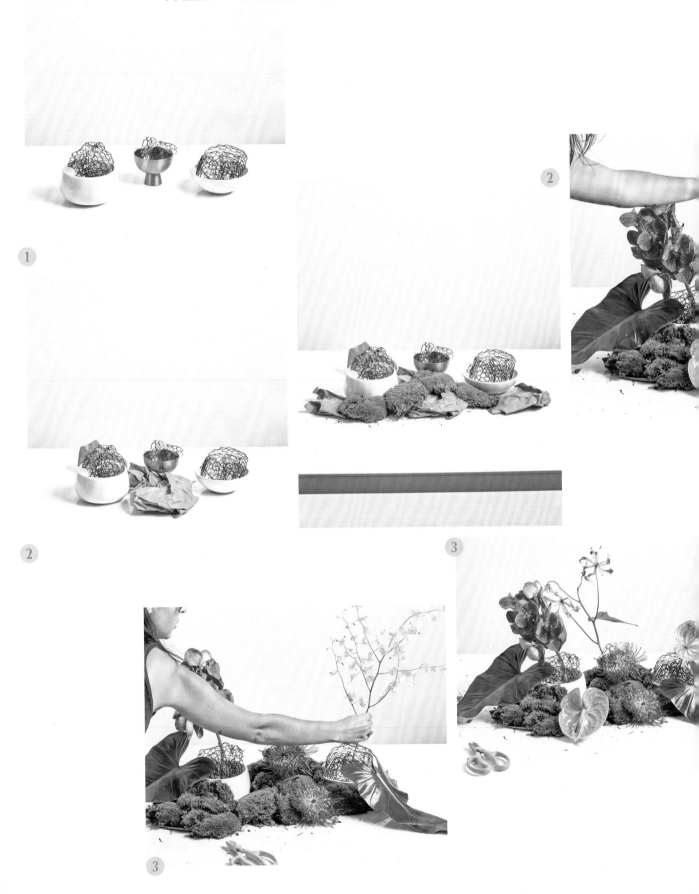

DESSERT PARTY

Playing with flowers doesn't have to mean stuffy, formal arrangements. It's fun to just mess around with leftover flowers and see what works! For this dessert table, I used various stems, desserts, and boas to create a grand party of flowers that feels wild, over-the-top, and busy in the best way. While you can buy flowers specifically for this look, this is one of those times when you can put all those leftover stems to work!

169

DESSERT PARTY

FLOWERS

9 stems anthurium
11 stems daisies
8 stems pampas grass
3 stems preserved and dyed pampas grass
3 preserved and dyed scabiosa pods
1 stem dried hydrangea

TOOLS

2 feather boas
Several kenzans in various widths
Floral putty

STEPS

1. Start by placing all your desserts out on the table and situating them where you know you'll want them. Then you can start building your tablescape around them.

2. Place the boas in a snakelike fashion, draping across the table, and start interspersing the kenzans randomly over the whole tabletop.

3. Start adding flowers, one by one. While the configuration is ultimately up to you, here are some ideas to get you started:

- A cluster of two anthuriums, one resting directly on a kenzan, concealing it from view, and another set into the kenzan and reaching high up from the table

- A few stems inserted directly into the desserts (avoid toxic plants and make sure not to ingest any part of the plant)

- A fanned-out configuration of several stems of pampas grass behind the desserts to create a sort of backdrop

- Anthuriums or hydrangea set directly on the surface

- Tall single-flower moments of preserved scabiosa pods or daisies angled out from the surface

INSTALLATIONS + HOME DECOR

There are other fun, creative ways to display florals in your home besides a single arrangement on top of a table. In this section, we explore some unique ways to do just that—whether for a party or just for your own personal enjoyment. These floral installations may seem complicated and hard to pull off, but I'm here to show you that with a few simple tools and tricks, you can easily create modern floral installations in your home. The fresh floral installations are best enjoyed for a short period, so I suggest making them for special occasions. The dried floral installations are meant to last, so find them a permanent place somewhere in your home!

PILLARS IN PINK

Asymmetrical floral pillars are one of my favorite floral arrangements to create because they don't require complicated, custom-built backdrops or heavy mechanics to ensure stability. In this modern rendition, I use a single flower variety for the bulk of the installation, which not only looks super chic and sophisticated but also makes sourcing and buying flowers a breeze. Just buy a few large boxes of hydrangeas from one location, rather than running around looking for a bunch of different varieties from a bunch of different vendors. These pillars would be the perfect backdrop for a photobooth, a small intimate backyard wedding, or your entryway for any at-home celebration. To support the flowers, use C-stands; these are normally used for photo equipment, but florists use them in situations like this, as they're relatively inexpensive, sturdy, and easy to buy online or rent from any photo rental place.

177

PILLARS
IN PINK

FLOWERS

70 stems hydrangea (see note)
1 box dyed preserved reindeer moss
25 stems carnations

TOOLS

2 C-stands
Chicken wire
Zip ties
Water tubes

~~~~~~

NOTE

Hydrangea → If you need long-lasting
pillars, use dried hydrangeas; they will
work just as well. Just skip the carnations.

Since my pillars were up against a wall, I
didn't worry about filling in the back. If
your pillars are going to live somewhere
where you'll be able to see the backs, just
double the stem counts on this list so
that you can fill in the backs as well.

STEPS

1. Set up the C-stands. The distance between them is up to you and your situation. Since my dog, Walter, was my only model, I kept the distance pretty narrow, with the pillars about 3 ft [1 m] apart.

2. Start wrapping the C-stands in chicken wire. To do this, measure out two pieces each as long as the C-stand is tall and wrap them around the C-stand. Use multiple zip ties to secure the chicken wire.

3. Before you start adding hydrangeas, cut the stems fairly short, approximately 4 in [10 cm], and place them in water tubes. With most other flowers, I'd tell you to skip this part if the install is meant to be up for only a few hours, but hydrangeas are really fickle and can die quickly!

4. Start adding hydrangeas to one C-stand. There isn't a specific method you need to follow, but make sure you're covering as much of the chicken wire as possible. Inevitably, there will be smaller holes left between the hydrangeas, which you'll cover up with carnations later, but try to cover up as much of the wire as you can at this stage. To create depth in the arch, place the hydrangeas in varying planes—that is, some blooms should be closer to the chicken wire than others.

5. Once you feel good about one side, start working on the other. You can always return to the first side for adjustments. It's helpful to take a step back and look at the installation from afar.

6. Once each side of the arch is pretty much full, start arranging the moss on the floor. Tuck some pieces under the lowest hydrangeas so that it feels integrated with the arch.

7. As a last step, fill in any remaining gaps with the carnations. I like to nestle them deep into the piece so they're not very noticeable.

5

5

6

5

5

7

7

GRASSY, CLASSY CLOUD

Floating floral clouds are easy to execute and create a major payoff. Floral clouds just make people happy. I mean, it makes sense! Who wouldn't love to look at a whimsical puff of suspended blooms? I imagine these floral clouds in a home setting, living above a dining table, over a bed, or even tucked into a cute corner of the house. For this rendition, I decided to use an assortment of ornamental grasses that are easy to forage in the summertime. While you're seeing them here in their fresh state, ornamental grasses will dry up similar to how they look fresh. The principles you'll learn here can be applied to essentially any bloom, dry or fresh. It's best to build this arrangement where it will be suspended. If you can't build it in its final place, try hanging it from a clothing rack and working on it there. Having it already hanging will make things like weight distribution and stem distribution easier.

GRASSY, CLASSY CLOUD

FLOWERS

50 stems ornamental grasses

TOOLS

Chicken wire

Fishing wire (see note)

Wall hook or Command picture-hanging strips

NOTE

Fishing Wire → Any string will work here, but I prefer fishing wire, as it's strong yet thin enough that you don't really see it.

STEPS

1. Create a ball of chicken wire, just under 12 in [30.5 cm] wide. You want the wire to be pretty tight—enough so you can easily stick a stem in one side and out the other—but not so tight that there aren't multiple entry points wide enough for the grasses.

2. Using fishing wire, hang the chicken wire ball. You can either hang it where it will ultimately live or do what I did: Hang it from a clothing rack, build it there, and then transfer it to its final display spot.

3. Start inserting stems, keeping weight distribution in mind—if you add a single stem to one side, balance it out by adding a stem to the other side. Otherwise you might find the cloud leaning one way or the other, which will just make it harder to build a steady, well-rounded cloud.

4. When placing stems, try to keep the overall shape round by adding stems on all sides. But also find points where you can introduce some irregularity for visual interest: Have one stem poking out a little farther on one side, or a stem at the bottom cascading down just slightly more than the others. This will make for a more organic cloud shape.

5. Once you've added stems all around, take a step back and adjust any spots that feel too heavy. For example, you might find that you added one too many stems to one side or that there's a bald spot on another.

6. Hang the cloud anywhere you'd like, using a wall hook or Command strips to secure the arrangement to the ceiling.

4

5

5

UNDER THE
DRIED PALMS

Earlier in this book, I mentioned that I very rarely make all-dried
arrangements. Well, the exception to that is home installations
like this one. Sometimes you want botanicals in your home that
last longer than a week. This is the time for dried palms and
pampas grasses to shine! Using a small grid panel as your base
makes this arrangement simple to assemble and easy to hang.

UNDER THE
DRIED PALMS

4 stems dried palm leaves
10 stems dried pampas grass
2 stems dried banksia

One 12 by 15¾ in [30.5 by 40 cm]
white grid panel
Command picture-hanging strips
Chicken wire
Zip ties

STEPS

1. Hang the grid panel on a wall using Command strips. It's best to build this install in place, as it might be a little challenging to move once it's put together.

2. Create a small ball of chicken wire, about 6 in [15 cm] wide. Attach the chicken wire ball to the bottom right corner of the grid panel using zip ties. The chicken wire ball will create more support for the heaviest part of the piece.

3. Arrange three palm leaves in the chicken wire, pointing to nine o'clock, eleven o'clock, and two o'clock. When inserting the stems, make sure there are multiple points of contact between the stem and the chicken wire and secure them in place with zip ties. Add the fourth palm leaf pointing toward five o'clock.

4. Start filling in the negative space with the pampas grass, inserting the stems into the chicken wire. I like to place the pampas grass at different depths of field, some in front and some behind the palm leaves. You can use single long stems or break up the single stems into smaller bunches by cutting the pampas stems in half.

5. Finish the piece by adding the dried banksia stems to the center.

UNDER THE DRIED PALMS

2

3

3

3

4

4

5

III.
RESOURCES + TIPS

I recommend shopping at your local garden shop or floral supply store when it comes to tools and vases. These businesses focus on a very specific market and are slowly disappearing due to competition from online shops. If you don't have local sources, here are some online shops that carry a lot of these supplies:

WHERE TO BUY YOUR TOOLS + VASES

AFLORAL www.afloral.com	Afloral is a great resource for trendy vases and dried florals.
JAMALI FLORAL + GARDEN SUPPLY www.jamaligarden.com	Jamali is my go-to source for vases. They have everything from trendy to classic and are constantly updating their stock.
LO FLORIST SUPPLIES www.lofloristsupplies.com	LO Florist Supplies is a no-frills shop for tools, vases, and vessels.
QUALITY WHOLESALE www.qualitywholesale.com	I shop Quality Wholesale in person, since it's located in Miami. They have a great selection of modern vases and always have a lot in stock!
MICHAEL'S www.michaels.com	In addition to their craft materials, Michael's has a lot of floral supplies. I run there when I'm in a pinch!
FLORAL SUPPLY SYNDICATE www.fss.com	Great for supplies and basic vases.

WHERE TO BUY YOUR FLOWERS

Local flower shops: Most cities have at least one local flower shop that sells premade arrangements, arrangements made to order, and loose flowers by the single stem. Flowers here will be marked up to retail, so they will definitely be more expensive than a wholesaler's, but it's a great way to buy single stems and also support your local florist.

Wholesalers: Florists buy their flowers from a wholesaler. Some wholesalers allow you to purchase by the bunch; others allow you to order in advance only in large quantities. Many wholesalers require a wholesale license in order to buy from them, but some are open to the public.

Flower markets: Most large cities will have a flower market where multiple vendors come together in one space (or street!) to sell flowers. Some of them are open to the public, but some require a wholesale license, so check before heading out.

Online floral suppliers: In the age of DIY, many online floral suppliers will ship to you. Most require a large minimum order.

Grocery stores: Grocery stores are a great place to buy flowers when you can't otherwise find them. Don't be put off by buying premade bouquets! Feel free to unwrap the bouquet and rearrange how you wish, pulling out the flowers you don't like and keeping only the ones you do!

Forage: While I'm not encouraging you to go snipping flowers in your neighbor's front garden, foraging is an option that many florists turn to for more unusual floral items than you can buy. The generally accepted rule is that you should never take more than you need or more than 10 percent of what's available, and definitely don't cut anything that's rare or endangered. However, bonus points if you're cutting common or noxious weeds. Just be careful of poisonous plants and flowers when you go snipping!

Transporting your arrangements requires patience and care! It's one of the most stressful parts of being a florist. All of a sudden, speed bumps and erratic drivers are your worst enemies. Still, sometimes you have to take an arrangement to a friend. Or sometimes the party is elsewhere! Here are some tips and tricks to get your arrangements from point A to point B with the least possible mess.

HOW TO TRANSPORT YOUR ARRANGEMENTS

1. **Pack them up.** The goal is to make the vase as stable as possible. If I still have the box the vase came in, I like to put the vase (florals and all!) back into the box. The flat bottom and enclosing walls of the box provide good support.

2. **Place them snugly in a crate or plastic container.** Once they're in their cardboard box, put the boxed arrangement in a plastic container or crate. You can even put a few in one crate to nestle them in really tightly, or pad with bubble wrap. This creates another layer of stability.

3. **Place them on a flat surface in the car.** Once they're ready to be packed into the car, place them on the flattest surface. This is usually the trunk or the floor. Unfortunately, seats aren't the best place to put them, as they're usually slightly curved and slanted. If you're able to, fold down the back seats to maximize that flat space.

4. **Drive slowly.** Lastly, drive slowly and steadily, or you might have spilled arrangements or water sloshing everywhere!

ACKNOWLEDGMENTS

My immense gratitude to Calma Floral's first customers and clients. Your trust in me gave me the confidence to know that even if I was figuring it out as I went, I was doing *something* right.

A *big* hug to all my friends, who have had to hear me talk about this for almost two years now. I'm so, so sorry. It's over now! Pati, thank you for sitting down with me at the very beginning and helping me outline what this book could look like. Jonathan, for opening up your space to me when I was in desperate need of somewhere to flower. Rosie, for being a second set of eyes during the design process. Denise and Christina, for your amazing baking skills (which you get to see in this book on pages 168-73 but which I really wish you could taste instead). Eden and Billy, for always planning the best getaways when I so desperately needed a break from work.

Shout-out to my first ever work mentors: Alex Pollack, Alex Grossman, and Adam Rapoport. We haven't worked together in a long time, but my years working under you all taught me so much that I carry with me to this day. And while I'm on the subject of old work buds, a huge shout-out to my old coworkers, many of whom have gone on to write their own amazing cookbooks and newsletters, and who have all lent me their knowledge as I worked through this book journey myself. Molly, Andy, Rachel, Rosie, Michele: You guys are the best! <3

Emma, thank you so much for shooting this book for me. I'm so happy that, even years after both of us left our desk jobs, we're still able to work together so closely. Shooting this with you has been an easy breezy dream! Alex and Michelle, thank you both for being a second set of hands at the shoots—your presence led to a calm, peaceful, and organized process!

So much gratitude for my agent, Michelle, who made the beginning stages of this process run smoothly and who ensured my book got into the right hands. And speaking of the right hands, I'm so, so thankful to have had such an amazing publishing team who trusted me and my vision. Claire and Lizzie, you both have made this entire process so fun and collaborative— there is no one else I would have rather worked with.

To all the flower girlz who have helped me build Calma into what it is. Particularly Gaby, who will forever be the OG Calma Flower Girl. And to Dunia, who has quickly become my right hand in everything I do—I wouldn't want to do it without you!

To Chaz, who has been with me on this flower journey since day one, providing support both mentally and physically (hire him to build your retail space!). I will never be able to put into words how grateful I am.

And to my family, who have always been there for me no matter what. Mom, Stephi, Abuela, Abuelo, Jeannie, Gina . . . I love you guys so much!

KEEP CALM(A) AND FLOWER ON . . .